Israel: God's Time Clock!

WHAT LIES AHEAD FOR the MIDDLE EAST, the UNITED STATES & ALL MANKIND?

By Dr. James Stuart Ford
(Bachelor of Theology, Bachelor of Arts, Master of Arts in Religion, and Doctor of Religious Education)

Copyright © 2008 by Dr. James Stuart Ford

Israel: God's Time Clock!
What Lies Ahead For the Middle East, the United States & All Mankind?
by Dr. James Stuart Ford

Printed in the United States of America

ISBN 978-1-60477-867-0

All rights reserved solely by the author. The author guarantees all contents are original and do not infringe upon the legal rights of any other person or work. No part of this book may be reproduced in any form without the permission of the author. The views expressed in this book are not necessarily those of the publisher.

Unless otherwise indicated, Bible quotations are taken from the Authorized King James Version. Copyright © 2003 by Thomas Nelson Inc.

www.xulonpress.com

Dedication

This book is dedicated to God the Father, God the Son, and God, the Holy Spirit. Second, it is dedicated to my precious wife and family members who helped in its writing. Last, but not least, it is dedicated to helping readers to understand the Word of God and be prepared for the earth shaking events of the "last days." Above all it is our prayer that all who read it who are unsaved will accept Jesus Christ as Savior and LORD!

Table of Contents

INTRODUCTION: *Why Write About the Nation of Israel?* ix
Chap. 1: *Why Israel Can Be Considered A Messenger!* 11
Chap. 2: *What Is Not True Concerning Israel: (1) The Body of Christ Church has replaced Israel. (2) Israel is really the United States and Great Britain* 19
Chap. 3: *Where Do We Stand At the End of the Age? Could This Be the Last Generation?* 27
Chap. 4: *The Three Days of Hosea* 35
Chap. 5: *The Battle of Gog and Magog (Ezek. Chaps. 38 & 39)* 41
   Part One: Who are the Invaders? 41
   Part Two: The Climax to the Invasion! 53
Chap. 6: *Israel in the Tribulation* 59
Chap. 7: *Where Will the Antichrist Come From? What Will Be His End? Why Many Will Worship Him!* 63

Chap. 8: *The Antichrist's Action's and God's Judgment!* 67
Chap. 9: *The False Prophet and the False Church* .. 71
Chap.10: *Signs of the End* 77
Chap.11: *Is the Antichrist Alive Today?* 81
Chap.12: *A Final Summary* 85

Introduction

Why Write About the Nation of Israel?

While, as will be shown, there are several reasons for writing about the Nation of Israel and the Jewish people, what the author feels is perhaps the primary reason is the fact that many, both learned and unlearned, seem in a real sense absolutely ignorant of the Bible's teaching. One example is the opinion expressed by many concerning Israel: "Jews are a bunch of shrewd, money making merchants who take advantage of ordinary people, especially in America. Thus the best thing is to have as little dealings with them as possible."

A second opinion, expressed by many, even those who are well educated Christians, is that Israel is responsible for the much of the past and present turmoil in the Middle East. A more recent example is the book: "Palestine: Peace Not Apartheid," by Jimmy Carter. A quote from the books introduction states: "There will be no substantive and permanent peace for any peoples in this troubled region as long as Israel is violating key U.N. resolutions, official American policy and the international 'road map' for peace, occupying Arab lands and oppressing the Palestinians." [1] While the book is interesting reading, it, like so many others on the same subject, fails to take into account what the Bible itself says about Israel and the land of Palestine, past, present and future.

In a nutshell, this is the purpose of this book.

---

1. Carter, Jimmy. *Palestine: Peace Not Apartheid.* NewYork: Simon & Shuster

Chapter One

Why Israel Can Be Considered a Messenger?

In answer to the opening question: Why Write About Israel? Many, especially Christians, will probably reply: "The nation of Israel is worth writing about because it is the nation in which the Lord Jesus Christ, the Savior of the world, was born, lived, ministered, and died upon the rugged cross of Calvary." It's message was given through Jewish writers for the benefit of all mankind. However, while these statements are absolutely true, there is more. In Deut. 32:8 we are told:

> *"When the most high divided to the nations their inheritance, when he separated the sons of Adam, he set the bounds of the people according to the number of the children of Israel."*

Genesis Chap. Ten gives us the account of this division of the nations which takes place after the death of Noah, and before the building of the Tower of Babel. Of course Israel, as a nation, only existed in the mind of God. The least that can be said concerning this thought-provoking verse (Deut. 32:8) is that it makes the reader ask "Why?"

As we study related Scripture it becomes quite clear that the people of the nation of Israel, the Jews, are special in God's sight and purpose. In Exodus 4:22 Moses is instructed to tell Pharaoh (the ruler of Egypt) *"Thus saith the Lord, Israel is my son, even my firstborn."* In Deut. 4 God gives the Ten Commandments to Israel and in the Scriptures that follow He allows kings to govern the nation and calls prophets to guide them spiritually.

Though this Jewish nation has always been located on a land-bridge between two continents, yet it seems quite small when compared to the rest of the nations. Likewise, its importance. However, what is evident from a study of the Old Testament and History is that there has been a force of some sort working to destroy this tiny, seemingly unimportant, nation. From Egypt, to Rome, to Hitler's Germany, attempts have been made to wipe this particular nation from the map of existence, with supposedly friendly nations showing but little concern. In our own time Arab Muslim leaders, such as the president of Iran, have expressed the same sentiment. Again the question is "Why?"

From Scripture we learn that the "Why?" is the force the Bible terms Satan, or the Devil. And, as we shall see, he is aware of God's purpose and plan for Israel and has been, and still is: determined to defeat it. Some will ask: Why does the Devil care about Israel? Surely this tiny nation is of little threat to the prince of darkness (Luke 4:5-8). Or is it? More later, but as the prophet Jeremiah tells us (Jer. 31:34-37): *If the*

Sun and Moon and Stars cease to exist, only then shall Israel cease from being a nation before me forever." If the devil can destroy Israel as a nation and a people, he will have made Almighty God a liar and the Bible unreliable. As already suggested, when we take time to study Bible History, the story of the Jewish people, past, present and future, occupies a great portion of Scripture. Other nations are mentioned, but only in the sense that they have dealings, good or bad, with Israel. All of the Bible's writings and prophecies, in both Testaments, are by and through Jewish writers. In the Old Testament all of the promises and covenants are in relation to Israel. In the New Testament all the offers of forgiveness and blessing are first offered to Jews (Scriptures such as Romans 1:16 and John 1:11 13 make this plain.) In Romans 1:16 Paul tells us:

"For I am not ashamed of the gospel of Christ: for it is the power of God unto salvation to everyone that believeth; to the Jew first and also to the Greek." This confirms John's promise:

"He came unto his own, and (they) received him not, but to as many as received him, to them gave he power to become the sons of God, even to them that believe on his name. Which were born, not of blood, nor of the will of the flesh, nor of the will of man, but of God.".

About 1921 B.C. God tells "Abram" (later changed to Abraham) the son of Terah who was a descendant of Shem (Gen.10: 11-26), who was the firstborn son of Noah(Gen. 9:18), to leave Haran in the land of the

Chaldees (Gen. 11:29-12:1). In response to his obedience, God makes a promise.

"...Get thee out thy country, and from thy kindred, and from thy father's house, unto a land that I will shew thee: And I will make of thee a great nation, and I will bless thee, and make thy name great; and thou shalt be a blessing: And I will bless them that bless thee, and curse him that curseth thee: <u>and in thee shall all families of the earth be blessed"</u> (Gen. 12: 1-3).

In Gen 15:13-14 we learn that God makes a covenant (with a promise) to Abraham that though his seed will be "a stranger" in a land that is not theirs (Egypt) and shall serve them; (and be afflicted 400 years) he will bring them out "with great substance." In Gen. Chap. 21, when Abraham is 100 years old and Sarah too old to become naturally pregnant (Gen. 18:12), Sarah, by God's blessing, conceives and gives birth to Isaac (the name signifies "laughter or delight").

To return to the story line of Gen. 15, what should be noted is that the account of the Passover and the Blood applied to the Door Posts (Ex. 12:11-14), pointed ahead to Calvary and the sacrificial death of the Lord Jesus Christ. In verses 18 to 21 of Gen.15, God adds to the covenant/promise: *"Unto thy seed have I given this land from the river of Egypt unto the great river, the river Euphrates...."*

In Gen.32:28 we learn that Jacob's name is changed to Israel (literally–a prince with God.).

In 1st Chronicles 2:1-2 the "sons of Israel" (12) are listed. In verse 3 the sons of Judah are given. The rest of the chapter (52 verses) lists the descendants of Judah to the time of David. In 1st Kings, chapters 11 and 12, we read of the rebellion of the house of Israel against the house of David (1st Kings 12:19-24). In Daniel Chapter One the reader is told of the invasion of Israel by the Babylonians (606 B.C.), and the taking of Daniel and many others into a period of captivity that would last 70 years. As will be considered later, Daniel is given several prophetic visions that look forward to the future and destiny of the Jewish nation and all of mankind.

Of course the most significant event in the history of Israel is the birth of the Messiah, the Christ child, whom the devil attempts to destroy by the hand of the wicked King Herod. The Gospels tell us, in much depth, about the life, death, and glorious resurrection of the Lord Jesus, whom Satan opposed almost every step of the way. While numbers of individual Jews accepted him as the Messiah, the nation, as a whole (especially its religious and political leaders), did not. As a result, in A.D.70, the Romans, who first occupied the nation in 63B.C., destroy Jerusalem and the Temple, putting to death a great number of the Jewish population, while numerous more are scattered among the nations of the world.

However, what is all important is that they continued to be Jewish and were not absorbed by the particular nations into which they were scattered.

And, as one studies both History and Scripture, it is apparent that the nation remains divided into two segments: that of Israel (the northern kingdom of ten tribes) and Judah and Benjamin (the southern kingdom) until one considers Ezek. Chap. 37. Here the reader is told that the time will come when the "dry bones" (the Jews scattered among all of the nations), will come to life (v.5); become clothed again with "sinews" (muscles) and flesh (v.6-8), and have the "breath of life" breathed into them (v.9). Verse eleven declares that they are "the whole house of Israel." Verses 12-14 state that this resurrected people will be restored to their "own land" and that God will "put his Spirit within them." In the rest of the chapter (verses 15-28) the prophet, Ezekiel, is told to take two sticks and write upon on one the name of "Israel" and upon the other the name "Judah." Then he is instructed to join the two sticks together to make "one stick." What is so significant about this passage of Scripture is: It has been partially fulfilled in our time (in the life time of the author and that of many readers). In 1948 (May15th) Israel declared itself, an official nation(one single nation representing all of the historic "12 tribes").

This fulfillment of the above prophecy, given a few years prior to 570 B.C. (well over 2500 years ago), has much to say about the amazing accuracy of Bible prophecy. Since so much of the Bible's prophecy concerning the end of this present age is related to Israel, these truths must be considered in this light. Understanding what God says about this nation and its people is <u>the key to understanding the future!</u> It is the author's conviction that there is a sense in which, along with the Word of God, the nation of Israel is God's Message and Time Clock to all mankind! Unfortunately, most of the news media, on T.V. and other wise, (except for a few Bible preachers) do not understand this important truth.

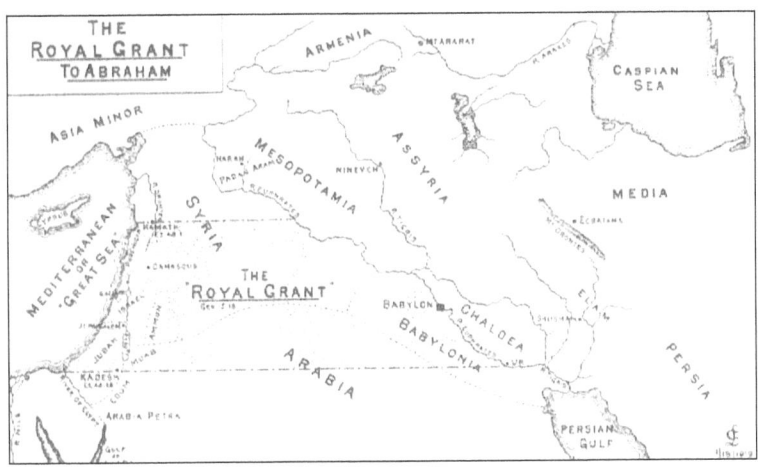

Royal Grant Map

The Land God Ordained For Israel

"In the same day the Lord made a covenant with Abraham saying, Unto thy seed have I given this land, from the river of Egypt unto the great river, the river Euphrates." (Gen. 15:18)

In Deuteronomy Chapter 33, just before his death (Chap. 34), God gives a promise to Moses concerning the nation of Israel and its future.

"The eternal God is thy refuge, and underneath are the everlasting arms: and he shall thrust out the enemy from before thee; and shall say, Destroy them. Israel then shall dwell in safety alone: the fountain of Jacob shall be upon a land of corn and wine; also his heavens shall drop down dew. Happy art thou, O Israel: who is like unto thee, O people saved by the LORD, the shield of thy help the sword of thy excellency!...thine enemies shall be found liars...thou shalt tread upon their high places."

Chapter Two

What Is Not True Concerning Israel

1. That the Body of Christ Church Has Replaced Israel.

Perhaps the greatest mistake made by preachers and Bible students today is that of Replacement Theology. This is the concept that despite the truth stated in the Introduction, the nation of Israel has been totally set aside in the program of God. This because Israel, as a nation, rejected Christ as the Messiah. Too often Bible prophecies related to Israel are twisted to apply to the Body of Christ church. One scripture offered as proof is 1st. Thess. 2:15-16. Here Paul states that because the Jews, as a nation,

> *"...killed the Lord Jesus, and their own prophets, and have persecuted us (Paul and others);.... Forbidding us to speak to the Gentiles that they might be saved.... wrath has come upon them to the uttermost."*

Other passages are Gal. 6:16, which refers to "the Israel of God." Gal. 3:28 states: "There is neither Jew nor Greek...for ye are all one in Christ Jesus;" and Eph. 2:14 which states:

"For he is our peace, who hath made both one, and hath broken down the middle wall of partition between us."

The phrase "all Israel will be saved" (Rom. 11:26) is said to refer to only the historic and ongoing conversion of Jews to Christianity. However, when one carefully considers all of Romans Chap. 11, the truth is made plain. While all born again Christians, both Jew and Gentile, become part of one spiritual body (1st Cor. 10:17; 12:12 and 27; Eph. 2:16 and 4:4), Israel still exists as a natural, human nation. Some, whom God foreknew (Rom. 11:2-12), have come to salvation through faith in Christ as Savior. The rest, as a nation, though blinded (spiritually-v.7), have only "stumbled;" they have not completely "fallen." Verses 11 through 33 of Rom. Chap. 11 make this truth indisputably plain. Verses 11 and 12 tell us:

"...Have they stumbled that they should fall? God forbid: but rather through their fall salvation is come unto the Gentiles, for to provoke them (Israel) to jealousy. Now if the fall of them be the riches of the world, and the diminishing of them the riches of the Gentiles, how much more their fullness (their return)?

Verse 15 adds: *"For if the casting away of them be the reconciling of the world, what shall the receiving of them be, but life from the dead?"*

As will be shown, a great world wide revival will come through the ministry of Jewish preachers who become "obedient Jonahs" (Zech. 8:23).

2. Israel Is Really The United States and Great Britain.

This is a rather unique teaching presented (as far as this author knows) first by Herbert W. Armstrong. Armstrong was the Pastor, in general, of the World Wide Church of God; Editor-in-chief of the Plain Truth magazine as well as president of Ambassador College in Pasadena, California (founded in 1947); as well as being the Chairman of an International, Charitable Organization known for humanitarian activities.

In a book, first published and copyrighted in 1967, and distributed free of charge, Armstrong goes to a great deal of effort in an attempt to prove from Scripture that the people, whom the world in general refers to as being "Jews" are only a minority of the world's true Jews. The truth, as proposed by Armstrong, is that the majority of true Jews are citizens and descendants of citizens of Britain and the United States.

Space does not permit a detailed examination and answer to Armstrong's theory, however an examination of Scripture in the Book of Revelation seems clearly to refute it.

In Rev. 7:1-8 we read of the sealing of the 144,000 which occurs just before "the great day of his (God's) wrath" described in Rev. 6:17. The 144,000 are distinctly named as 12,000 from each of the 12 tribes of "the children of Israel." The Tribes named are Judah, Reuben, Gad, Asher, Naphtali, Manasseh, Simeon, Levi, Issachar, Zebulon, Joseph and Benjamin. Later they are seen in Heaven (Rev. 14:1-5), evidently caught up after preaching and bringing to the Lord *"...the great multitude, which no man could number."* (Rev. 7:9)

That all of these twelve tribes existed as such in the Acts period, and were then known by name is made clear by the Apostle Paul in Acts 26:7 Here Paul states that he had lived as a strict Pharisee (v.5), and was of the very same "hope"(of the fulfillment of the promised Messiah's coming), as were the "twelve tribes" who were then "serving God day and night." What is made plain is that the twelve tribes were then living in the land of Israel and were recognized as such, and were very dedicated to keeping the Old Testament Laws. They had not, as yet, been scattered among the nations. This truth is verified by the Apostle James in a letter addressed primarily to the "twelve tribes." *"James a servant of God, and of the LORD Jesus Christ, to the twelve tribes, which are scattered abroad, greeting"* (James 1:1).

In Rev. 21 we see a picture of "that great city, the holy Jerusalem, descending out of heaven from God...." This heavenly city, often called the "new Jerusalem" has a wall with 12 gates on which are written: "the names of the twelve tribes of the children of Israel." What should be noted is that if the names of the so called "lost ten tribes" were changed to Great Britain and the United States, no one told God about it.

3. Israel of the Bible is Really the Present Day Jehovah Witness Movement

Another false teaching is that the 12 tribes, so clearly distinguished in Rev. 7:4-8, refer to the first 144,000 Jehovah Witnesses that were saved and became known as "dedicated witnesses." In verse 4 of Rev. 7 it plainly declares that those "sealed (selected)" are *"of all the tribes of the children of Israel."* Though this seems clear enough to rule out any Witnesses not Jewish,, verse 4 of Rev. 14 declares that all of these 144.000 individuals are said to be not only Jewish, but male virgins. It reads:

"These are they which were not defiled with women, for they are virgins. These are they which follow the Lamb... being the first fruits unto God and the Lamb. And in their mouth was found no guile: for they are without fault before the throne of God."

If this scripture looks back to the first Gentiles saved, then it cannot refer to the Witness Movement since it did not come into being until the early 1870's (See Jehovah's Witnesses, Who Are They? What Do They Believe?: WATCH TOWER, 25 Columbia Heights, Brooklyn NY 11201-2483). If the passage looks forward to the first Jews saved during the coming Tribulation period (as it possibly does), the Witness Movement is again a misfit. They are guilty of changing Scripture to boost their movement, forgetting the "judgment" of God pronounced on those who "add to, or take away" from God's Word (Rev. 22:18 -19). It reads:

> *"For I testify unto every man that heareth the words of the prophecy of this book, If any man shall add unto these things, God shall add unto him the plagues...written in this book."*

4. Israel Stole the Land They Occupy!

Many who side with the Palestinians in the present Israeli/Palestinian conflict do so because they feel that when the Jews became an official nation in 1948, the territory they occupied actually belonged to the Palestinians. What they fail to realize is that Israel's presence in the land is a fulfillment of both prophecy and promise. Genesis 15:18-21 states:

> *"In the same day the Lord made a covenant with Abram saying, <u>Unto thy seed have I given the land</u> from the river of Egypt unto the great river, the river Euphrates: {the land of the} Kenites, and the Kenizzites, and the Kadmonites, and the Hittites, and the Perizzites, and the Rephaim, and the Amorites, and the Canaanites, and the Girgashites, and the Jebusites."*
>
> Gen 17:7 and 8 promise: *"And I will establish my covenant between me and thee {Abram}, and thy seed after thee in their generation for <u>an everlasting covenant</u>....And I will give unto thee and thy seed after thee...<u>all</u> the land of Canaan for <u>an everlasting possession</u>; and I will be their God."*

It should be noted that in Gen. 15:13 God tells Abram that the nation of Israel will be afflicted in the land of Egypt four hundred years. At that time God will judge

Egypt and Israel will come out having *"spoiled the Egyptians."* The spoil was material wealth of *"jewels of silver, (and) of gold, and raiment."*

Israel, except for the 70 year Babylonian Captivity, occupied the land promised to them until A.D.135 when they were scattered among the nations by the Romans. This period of over 1300 years in which Israel occupied the land, seems to be the proof of their original possession. While they would be scattered among the nations, with large numbers put to death, this would be due to their rejection of the Lord Jesus as their promised Messiah.

To return to the Old Testament, in Numbers 34:1-12 a detailed description of the four borders of the Land of Canaan is given. In Deut.11:21-25 God promises Israel that if they will *"...diligently keep {His} commandments...to do them, to love the Lord your God, to walk in all his ways, and to cleave unto him; Then will the Lord drive out all these nations before you, and ye shall possess greater nations...mightier than yourselves. Every place whereon your feet shall tread shall be yours: from the wilderness and Lebanon, from the river Euphrates, even unto the uttermost sea shall your coast be."*

Joshua 21:43 tells the reader *"And the Lord gave unto Israel all the land which he sware (promised) unto their fathers, and they possessed it, and dwelt therein."*

Finally, in Ezekiel 37:21 to 24, God declares that He will *"...take the children of Israel from among the heathen...and gather them on every side and bring them into their own land; And I will make them one nation... upon the mountains of Israel and one king(one ruler) shall be king to them all:.."* (v.21).

In closing, note that verse 21 promises to *"bring them into their own land!"* Even when they were not there and scattered abroad, God reserved the land for them. As we will see, this is because God has a special place and purpose for "his people."

In closing, note that verse 24 looks forward to the time when *"David shall be their King."* This verse is another argument disputing "replacement theology," for if the Body of Christ Church has replaced Israel, as a "special purpose people," How can a resurrected David be a future king over a people who no longer exist?

When verses 24 thru 28 are considered it is wonderfully plain that God has declared Israel will be his people "for ever."

"And they shall dwell in the land that I have given unto Jacob my servant, wherein your fathers have dwelt; and they shall dwell therein, even they and their children, and their <u>children's children for ever:</u> and my servant <u>David shall be their prince forever"</u> (v.25).

"My taberacle also shall be with them: yea I will be their God, and they shall be my people" (v.27).

And the heathen shall know that I the Lord do sanctify <u>Israel, when my sanctuary shall be in the midst of them for ever more" (v.28).</u>

Chapter 3

Where Do We Stand as to the End of the Age? Could This Be the Last Generation?

When an attempt is made to answer the first question: Where do We Stand as to the End of the Age?, it will be helpful to first explain what is meant by "Age." While looking in a dictionary will reveal several definitions for the term "age," the definition in view at this point is "a distinct, historical period" (The American Century Dictionary). In relation to the Bible such a period of time is generally designated by many to be "a Dispensation." While all may not agree, many Bible scholars divide the history of man into seven such primary periods. These are: Innocence, Conscience, Human Government, Promise, Law, Grace, and Kingdom.

INNOCENCE was the period from Adam and Eve's creation until their sin of eating the forbidden fruit. CONSCIENCE covered the next period of time until the flood of Noah's day (Gen. 6 & 7). This period was followed by one termed HUMAN GOVERNMENT, which lasted until the building and destruction of the Tower of Babel (Gen. 8 to 11). The fourth dispensation has been termed PROMISE, which covered the bondage of the Jewish nation in Egypt for 400 years until the dispensation of the LAW (Ten commandments, given to the nation through Moses). The Dispensations of Promise and Law were then followed by the present dispensation of GRACE, commonly called the "church age." This will be followed by the Tribulation and then, the Millennial Reign, or the 1000 year KINGDOM age.

To return to the initial question: "Where Do We Stand as to the end of this Age (GRACE)?" Much could be presented, such as a study of the Seven Churches of Revelation (Chapters Two and Three), with each church representing a time period and the suggestion that the church is now in the last period. This is the Laodicean, or "lukewarm" age. *"I know thy works, that thou art neither cold nor hot: I would that thou were cold or hot. ....because thou art lukewarm...I will spue thee out of my mouth."* (However, many Christians feel the world-wide church is far from being "lukewarm," and thus, this scripture does not apply.)

Nevertheless, the clearest prophetic statement is found in the very words of the Lord Jesus himself as recorded in Luke 21:24-33. Verse 24 reads:

"And they (Israel) shall fall by the edge of the sword, and shall be led away captive into all nations: and Jerusalem shall be trodden down of the Gentiles, until the times of the Gentiles be fulfilled." (Under

the oppression of Hitler over six million Jews were put to death.)

The following verses (25-27) describe end time conditions of turmoil and fear that will be followed by the visible return of the Lord *"in power and great glory."*

In verse 28 the Lord exhorts: *"...when these things begin to come to pass, look up for your redemption draweth nigh."*

This command and warning is repeated again in verse 31. Then in verses 32 and 33 an important key declaration is given:

Verily I say unto you, This generation shall not pass away, till all be fulfilled. Heaven and earth shall pass away: but my words shall not pass away."

The above declaration is also given in Mat. 24:34 and Mk. 13:30. What is in view, it seems, is the "last generation," or the seventh dispensation. Above all, what seems vitally important to understand is that the Lord Jesus, our all wise, all knowing God, is saying that the generation that witnesses the return of the Jewish nation from a world wide scattering, and the restoration of Jerusalem to their control, will not come to an end until all the events spoken of in the entire chapter, including the Lords literal, visible return, are fulfilled.

In 1948 Israel again became an official nation. In 1967 they gained control of Jerusalem. Thus, it seems, the Lord has promised that many, who were born in 1967, will still be living when the events of the Rapture, the Tribulation, and the Lord's Second Coming are fulfilled! This leaves only a few years, at most, on the time clock, if we count a Biblical generation as being, at the most, 80 years (Psalm 90:10).

"The days of our years are threescore years and ten; and if by reason of strength they be fourscore years, yet ... it is soon cut off and we fly away."

Thus 1967, plus 80, brings us to the year 2047. Subtracting 7 years for the time of the Tribulation, the "few years" at the most are only 33 (at the time of this writing: 2007). During this time the Battle of Gog and Magog must occur, as well as the Rapture, and the formation of a World Government with the Antichrist as it head. For those who ask: "Why must the Rapture occur?" It is the author's conviction that the Body of Christ Church must be removed by the power of the Holy Spirit in order for the Antichrist to come to power (2nd Thess. 2:3-9).

"Let no man deceive you by any means: for that day shall not come (The Tribulation), except there come a falling away first, and that man of sin be revealed, the son of perdition; Who opposeth and exalteth himself above all that is called God, or is worshiped; so that as God sitteth in the temple of God, showing himself that he is God" (v.3&4).

Verses 7 thru 9 continue: *"For the mystery of iniquity doeth already work: only he that now letteth will let, until he be taken out of the way"*(v.7). (It should be noted that in Greek the word "letteth" means " restrain.") This special one who "letteth," or restrains, is the Holy Spirit. Certainly the Holy Spirit will not leave without taking the Body of Christ church with him. Two scriptures that seem clearly to prove this are Jude 14 and also Col. 3:4. They tell us that the Lord Jesus will bring with him the "saints," or "born again" believers, when He returns.

"*When Christ, who is our life, shall appear, then shall ye also appear with him in glory*" (Col. 3:4). "*And Enoch also, the seventh from Adam, prophesied of these saying, 'Behold, the Lord cometh with ten thousand of his saints'*" (Jude 14).

2nd Thess. 2:8 tells us: "*And then shall that wicked be revealed, whom the Lord shall consume with the spirit of his mouth, and shall destroy with the brightness of his coming: Even him, whose coming is after the working of Satan with all power and signs and lying wonders.*"

Rev. 13 tells us: "*And I stood upon the sand of the sea, and saw a beast rise out of the sea, (the sea of nations) having seven heads and ten horns, and upon his horns ten crowns, and upon his heads the name of blasphemy*" (v.1). Verse 3 continues: "*And I saw one of his heads as it were wounded to death; and his deadly wound was healed: and all the world wondered after the beast.*"

Here is a description of one of the amazing ways in which the Antichrist will deceive all of unsaved mankind: <u>by duplicating the resurrection of the Lord Jesus</u>.. This will be on world wide TV, Radio and in every newspaper. While we are told that the False Prophet will do many miracles, such as causing "*fire (to)come down from heaven on the earth in the sight of men*" (Rev. 13:11-15), this miraculous resurrection will be, without doubt, the greatest miracle of all (Rev. 13: 1-14).

In all probability the ten horns refer to a special, end time, ten nation federation. That this federation will be composed of ten nations that existed within the boundaries of the Old Roman Empire is made clear from Daniel 9:24 - 27

"Know therefore and understand that from the going forth of the commandment to restore and to build Jerusalem unto Messiah the Prince shall be seven weeks, and threescore and two weeks: the street shall be built again, and the wall, even in troublous times. And after threescore and two weeks shall Messiah be cut off, but not for himself: and the people of the prince that shall come shall destroy the city and the sanctuary, and the end thereof shall be with a flood, and unto the end of the war desolations are determined. And he (the Antichrist) shall confirm the covenant with many for one week (7 years): and in the midst of the week (after 3 and one half years) he shall cause the sacrifice (the worship of Jehovah) and the oblation (offerings) to cease, and for (with) the overspreading of abominations (an image of himself) he shall make it desolate, (true Temple worship) even until the consummation, and that determined shall be poured upon the desolate (desolator). (See 2ⁿᵈ Thess. 2:4.)

Most scholars agree this decree refers to that made by Artaxerxes to Ezra in 457 B.C. (EZRA 7:11-26). THE KEY IS: *"the people of the prince that shall come shall destroy the city and the sanctuary."* History tells us that these "people" were the Romans. Thus the Antichrist will come from a federation that will, in a sense, be a revived Roman Empire, or a European Union. History also tells us that the weeks are weeks of years and are divided into two periods. The first was a decree authorizing the rebuilding of Jerusalem and its wall (Nehemiah 2). It is dated in the Jewish month of Nisan 445 B.C.. The time from 445 B.C. until Palm Sunday just before the crucifixion of Jesus was 62 weeks of years, each year one of 360 days. (Numerous Bible passages show each month to be one of 30 days: Gen. 7:11 with 8:4; 7:24 with 8:3; Rev. 12:6, 7, 13 and 14). After an unknown time gap (the present church age) the 70th week of seven years will begin. The following chapter, relating to "The Three Days of Hosea," gives additional testimony to this time element.

Chapter 4

The Three Days of Hosea

Hosea, the first of the Minor Prophets, loves Gomer, an unfaithful wife. The story is a dramatic and prophetic portrayal of Jehovah's relationship with Israel, the favored nation. Given during the reign of Jeroboam II (786-746 BC), it reflects both future judgment and the declaration of Paul in Rom. 11: 25-27, that in due time (God's time) Israel will be delivered from "blindness," and restored to divine fellowship *("..And so all Israel shall be saved....")*. In addition, a unique time table is provided when Chapter 3 is linked to chapters 5 and 6 (5:15-6:1-3).

"For the children of Israel shall abide many days without a king, and without a prince, and without a sacrifice, and without an image, and without an ephod, and without teraphim: Afterward shall the children of Israel return, and seek the Lord their God, and David their King: and shall fear the LORD and his goodness in the latter days" (vs. 4-5).

The terms "king and prince" speak of the lack of a ruling monarch of any kind. A nation without a government is, in a real sense, a non-nation. "Without a sacrifice" refers to the lack of any type of God ordained, regular worship. (No temple with an altar on which to offer sacrifices.) On the other hand, the reference to "image...ephod, and teraphim" seems a declaration that during this time period the nation of Israel would never again worship idols.

A study of history relates that she became a nation in peril when she began a revolt against the Romans in 70 A.D.. When the revolt was put down over a million Jews were slain, and the Temple and its system of worship destroyed. Jews not killed, or made prisoners, were scattered among many nations. By 105 A.D. Israel no longer existed as an official nation, but simply as "Jews" only. As history records, they were mercilessly persecuted and often slain in the lands into which they retreated; but, as predicted, they did not take up the worship of the false gods of these nations.

A clue as to the length of the "many days" of verse 4, is found in verse 5 where Hosea tells us: *"afterward shall the children of Israel return* (to the special land), *and seek the LORD their God...and his goodness in the latter days."* This is when Israel again becomes a recognized, political nation. Not only has the return begun, it has not ceased and continues to this very day. Eliezer Braun, a Jewish writer, stated in the SHUVA ISRAEL NEWSLETTER: "Since the declaration of Statehood in 1948, Israel's population... increased from 600,000 to over 5 million in 2002....The Bible refers more than 700 times to the restoration of the Jewish people to the land of Israel. Despite five major wars, continual terrorism and constant international pressure to relinquish parts of our Biblical homeland, we continue to absorb new waves of immigrants from all over the world." (vol.

1, Issue # 12, Sept. 2000.) Reports show hundreds more have made "alyiah" or immigration, despite the increased intensity of the attacks of the Palestinian militants against Israeli sites. This is due, in part, to the financial support being extended by Jewish organizations to aid those who desire to come, but lack funds. Some may ask: Where do these Jewish groups get their money? It seems evident that God has given it to them to fulfill his Word. Despite centuries of persecution and ridicule by many, one characteristic of a "Jew" is that of a "rich merchant". An article in MIDNIGHT CALL (Sept. 2003), entitled "Jews and Money" by Wilfred Hahn, points out that Roget's Thesaurus lists the word 'Jew' as a synonym for...'wealthy'." In addition, "...one-third of American multi-millionaires are Jewish; and, the percentage of Jew households with (yearly) incomes greater than $50,000 is double that of non-Jews." This is an initial fulfillment of Bible prophecy that the Special Nation will not only be returned to their Special Land, but they will be blessed with Peace and Prosperity. Several scriptures make this future prophecy plain, but a detailed account is given in Isaiah, Chapters 60, 61, and 62. In brief: The time will come when Israel will be *"no longer forsaken and hated...(but) an eternal excellency,...they shalt also suck the milk of the Gentiles, (drain them of their wealth),... and thou shalt know that I the LORD am thy Savior and thy Redeemer, the mighty One of Jacob"* (Isaiah 60: 15-16).

To return to Hosea, in 5:15 the LORD says: *"I will go and return to my place, till they acknowledge their offense and seek my face: in their affliction they will seek me early."*

In chapter six, verses 1-3 the prophet puts words in the mouths of those who desire to return to the land:

"Come, and let us return unto the LORD: for he hath torn, and he will heal us, he hath smitten, and he will bind us up. After two days will he revive us: <u>in the third day he will raise us up, and we shall live in his sight.</u> Then shall we know, if we follow on to know the LORD: his going forth is prepared as morning; and he shall come unto us as the rain, as the latter and former rain unto the earth."

The questions are: When did the Lord turn away from Israel and leave them to be afflicted? How long are the two days? When did, or when will, the "third day" begin? Finally, how is he going to come unto them as "rain"? Didn't this happen on the Day of Pentecost?

In answer to the above: While Israel was scattered among the nations, beginning in 70 A.D., Paul tells us in I Thess. 2:14-16 (written 55 A.D.) that *"...wrath is come upon them to the uttermost."* This because they *"...killed the LORD Jesus, and their own prophets, and... persecuted us (Paul and his companions)....Forbidding us to speak to the Gentiles that they might be saved...."* Paul's statement seems to indicate that judicial judgment had already been pronounced. If one uses a 360 day/year calendar (as indicated in Gen. 7:11 and 8:3-5), and 1000 years as "one day" in God's plan (Ps. 90:4 and 2nd Pt. 3:8), and, if we count leap years, the time between 55 A.D. and 2008 is about 20 years short of the 2 days (two thousand years) which must be completed before the "third day" begins. If one considers Luke 21:24: *"...Jerusalem will be trampled under foot by the*

Gentiles until the times of the Gentiles be fulfilled," it seems quite likely that the year 1947, when, after nearly 2000 years, Jerusalem again became Israel's capital, was a sign pointing to Israel's " raising up"(turning to Christ) that will take place in the "third day." As will be shown in the chapter describing the Battle of Gog and Magog, this wonderful revival may be closer than many of us think!

Joel, Chapter Two, sheds light on the promise of Hosea 6:3 that, if Israel will *"follow on to know the Lord,"* he will rain upon them spiritually. The prophet promises (v.20) that after the defeat of the "northern army" (Gog and her allies as described in Ezek. 38 and 39), that *"he will cause to come down... the rain, the former rain, and the latter rain..."(v.23)....And it shall come to pass that whosoever shall call upon the name of the LORD shall be delivered: for in mount Zion and in Jerusalem shall be deliverance, as the LORD hath said, and in the remnant whom the Lord shall call" (v.32).*

Ezek. 36:26 - 28 tells us that after the Special People are restored to their Special Land, that then the Lord will *"cleanse them,"* providing both a new heart and spirit, and they will be *"The Priests of the LORD"* (Isa. 61:6). This is confirmed by Zech. 8:23. *"Thus saith the Lord of hosts; In those days it shall come to pass that ten men shall take hold, out of all languages of the nations, even shall take hold of the skirt of him that is a Jew. saying, We will go with you: for we have heard that God is with you."*

Thus, at last, "Jonah the Jew" will be obedient and fulfill the Special Nation's original calling. Sent to preach to Nineveh, capital of the then Gentile world, Jonah boarded a merchant ship going the other way.

Because of his disobedience God sent a great storm which did not cease until Jonah told the men of the ship to cast him into the sea. Though reluctant they complied with Jonah's request. As a result the storm ceased.

However when cast into the midst of the sea, Jonah was swallowed by a "great fish" (a type of the Gentile nations). Here he experienced the pains of hell (a type of Jewish persecution), and cried out for deliverance. Upon reaching dry land (Israel back in their land), Jonah was obedient and preached to Nineveh. The entire city repented and turned to the LORD (Jonah 3: 5-10). As a result of the Special Nation finally accepting Jesus Christ, the Special Person, as their LORD and Savior, not only will some be saved, but the entire nation (Jer. 31:33-34). However, before this wonderful time the Special Nation must endure more of Satan's attempts to destroy her. Perhaps very soon, the attempt by Gog and her Muslim allies. This will be discussed in the following chapter.

Chapter 5

The Battle of Gog and Magog (Ezek. Chaps. 37-39)

– Part One: Who Are the Invaders?

And the word of the Lord came unto me saying, Son of man, set thy face against Gog, the land of Magog, the chief prince of Meshech and Tubal, and prophecy against him, And say, Thus sayeth the Lord God; Behold, I am against thee...And I will turn thee back, and put hooks into thy jaws, and I will bring thee forth, and all thine army, horses and horsemen, all of them clothed with all sorts of armor, even a great company with bucklers and shields, all of them handling swords: Persia, Ethiopia, and Libya; all of them with shield and helmet; Gomer, and all his bands; the house of Togarmah of the north quarters, and all his bands: and many people with thee. (Chap. 38:1-6)

Chap. 39:1-6 states:

"*Therefore, thou son of man, prophesy against Gog, and say, thus saith the Lord God; behold,*

I am against thee O Gog, the chief prince of Meshech and Tubal: And I will turn thee back, and leave but the sixth part of thee (five-sixths will be destroyed), and will cause thee to come up from the north parts, and will bring thee upon the mountains of Israel: and I will smite thy bow out of thy left, and will cause thine arrows to fall out of thy right hand. Thou shalt fall upon the mountains of Israel, thou and all thy bands, and the people that is with thee: I will give thee unto the ravenous beasts of every sort, and to the beast of the field to be destroyed. Thou shalt fall upon the open field: for I have spoken it, saith the Lord God. And I will send a fire on Magog, and among them that dwell carelessly in the isles: and they shall know that I am the Lord." (Chap. 39:1-6)

The above verses sum up an account of what seems clearly to refer to an invasion of the land of Israel by a force from the north. This follows the prophecy of Chapter 37 that relates how the Jewish nation, though in a sense, both physically and spiritually dead and scattered among the nations as "dry(dead)bones," will be gathered together and have life breathed into them and will be brought unto the land of Israel (v. 1-14).

Though the twelve tribes of Israel were united in one nation under David (ca. 1000 B.C.), approximately 70 years later they were divided into the two weaker kingdoms of Israel (10 tribes) and Judah (2 tribes). However, in Ezekiel 37: 15-22 God tells the prophet to take two sticks (of wood) and write upon one "Israel" and upon one "Judah." Then he is told to join the two sticks together and make them one.

"....Thus saith the Lord God, Behold, I will take the children of Israel from among the heathen, whither they begone, and will gather them on every side, and bring them into their own land. And I will make them one nation in the land upon the mountains of Israel; and one king (ruler) shall be shall be king to them all: and they shall no more be two nations, neither shall they be divided into two kingdoms anymore at all (v.21 & 22)"

While some may feel this is yet future, it seems clear from what has been shown that Israel is back in the "special land" God promised to them as a "special, united (one stick) people" whom the Lord will use for a "special purpose.". However, as suggested, Satan still desires to destroy them and defeat God's purpose. In this chapter we will deal with this Satanic attempt which may be just around the corner. This is an attack upon Israel by Russia aligned with other Israel hating nations. Because there exists some difference of opinion by writers, past and present, as to the identity of these invaders, as well as the nature, and time of the invasion, it seems worthwhile to take a quick look at some of these concepts.

Let us begin with Matthew Henry's opinion expressed in his *"Commentary on the Whole Bible"* on page 1073 (published 1961 by Zondervan, Grand Rapids, Michigan). Henry stated that it is "highly unlikely" that the O.T. prophecy of the "two sticks" becoming "one stick" points to the Jewish nation becoming a single nation uniting all twelve of the historical tribes. Rather "it is a type of the uniting of Jews and Gentiles, Jews and Samaritans, in Christ and His church." However, since the apostle Paul tells us the Body of Christ Church is a mystery (Rom. 16:25;

Gal. 1:11-12) not revealed to any in the Old Testament, then Henry's theory is mistaken.

On the other hand, while Henry feels Ezek. 38 and 39 are fulfilled in the birth of the Christian Church, Jimmy Swaggart, (in his *Expositor's Bible* –Jimmy Swaggart Ministries, Baton Rouge, LA), expresses the conviction that all that is said of Gog and Magog looks forward to the battle of Armageddon spoken of in Rev.16:16. However, as can be shown, Armageddon is not a battle between a few specified nations, rather it is between *"the kings of the earth and the whole world"* (gathered together by Satan) to oppose Christ and the armies of heaven at his Second Coming (*"the battle of that great day of God Almighty"*—Rev.16: 14-16 and Rev. 19:11-21).

If the attack against Israel by Gog, as described in Ezek.38 and 39, is the same as that of the attack of the *"kings of the earth and the whole world"* upon the returning *"KING OF KINGS AND LORD OF LORDS,"* the description of the two conflicts, as well as that of the participants, seem clearly not to be the same. Therefore it is the author's conviction that neither of the above concepts are true. Yet, while the attack of Israel by Gog has nothing to do with the Body of Christ Church, it will be shown that it is a literal event that is separate from, and will take place before Armageddon. It is also interesting to note that in *The Holy Bible From Ancient Eastern Manuscripts,*(Published by A. J. Holman Co., Philadelphia, PA) the editor and translator, George M. Lamsa, suggests Magog is China and that God will send "a fire on those who dwell carelessly in Mongolia." While China seems not to have a religious hatred for Israel, without doubt, she would love to control the wealth of the Middle East Oil. However, when one considers the names of the allies of the chief invader (Magog), it would seem to eliminate China, as well as the direction from which the invaders come. (It is hard to conceive of China being north of Israel.)

The author's suggestion that the invasion of Israel by Magog (a "northern army") may be Russia is found by considering Ezekiel 38:2. As given in the New American Standard Bible, it reads: *"Son of man set thy face against Gog, the land of Magog, the chief prince of Rosh, of Meshech and Tubal."* The word "Rosh" seems quite possibly to be a reference to Russia, with Meshech and Tubal being two of Russia's primary cities.

However, Ezekiel tells us that he was not the first to prophesy of the invasion of Israel by a force from the north.

"Thus saith the Lord God; Art thou he of whom I have spoken in old time by my servants, the prophets of Israel, which prophesied in those days many years that I would bring thee against them? (Ezek. 38:16).

The above is a reference to Joel, who prophesied in the 8th century B. C., at least 200 years prior to the prophet Ezekiel. Joel, Chap. 2 tells the reader of an invading army, described as *"...a great people and a strong: there hath not ever been the like, neither shall be any more after it, even to the years of many generations" (v.2).* Verse 6 states: *"Before their face the people shall be much pained: all faces shall gather blackness (be filled with fear).*

Verses 7 thru 10 describe the invaders who will *"... run like mighty men:...climb the wall like men of war... shall not break ranks....Neither shall one thrust another {but} walk every one in his own path; when they fall upon the sword they shall not be wounded. They shall run to and fro in the city; they shall climb upon the wall; they shall climb upon the houses; they shall enter in at the windows like a thief. The earth shall quake before them; the heavens shall tremble; the sun and the moon shall be dark, and the stars shall withdraw their shining.."* Verse 11 declares the Lord *"shall utter his voice before his army: for his camp is very great and very terrible; and who can abide it?*

Here the Lord, refers to the invaders as *"his army"* because, they will fulfill his purpose, though all do not agree to the nature of the invaders with many believing they are simply the locusts spoken of in Chapter One. To others, the nature of the invaders appears to be almost that of robots propelled by remote control. (Pictures and information showing that the U.S. government has developed such equipment have been published, and it is probable that if the U.S. has developed such military power, Russia has done the same). However, it is doubtful that *"ravenous birds...and beasts of the field"* can *"devour"* the bodies of robots (39:4). Whatever the case, only one sixth of the invaders will be able to flee (39:2) and Israel will be divinely delivered. This promise comes in verses 12-thru 20 (See Joel: Chapter Two)in which the LORD declares: if Israel will *"turn to him with all your heart... with fasting...weeping...and mourning,"* that He will *"remove far off from you the northern army, and drive them into a land barren and desolate, with his face toward the east sea, and his hinder part toward the utmost sea, and his stink shall come up, and his ill savor shall come up, because he hath done great things."*

Verses 11 thru 20 of Joel 2 make plain God's purpose in allowing the invasion. It is to bring the nation of Israel to a place of repentance. In verse 11 the invasion is referred to as: *"the day of the Lord (that is) great and very terrible; and who can abide it?* In verses 12 and 13 Israel is told *"...turn ye even to me with all your heart, and with fasting, and with weeping, and with mourning: ... rend your heart, and not your garments, and turn unto the Lord your God: for he is gracious and merciful, slow to anger, and of great kindness, and repenteth him of the evil."* (God regrets what was necessary for Him to do in order to bring the nation to a place of repentance and fellowship.)

In verses 15 to 17 the nation is told to: *"Blow the trumpet in Zion, sanctify a fast, call a solemn assembly: Gather the people, sanctify the congregation, assemble the elders, gather the children, and those that suck the breast: let the bridegroom goeth forth of his chamber, and the bride out of her closet (dressing room). Let the priests, the ministers of the Lord, weep between the porch and the altar (of the temple), and let them say, Spare thy people, O Lord, and give not thine heritage to reproach, that the heathen (the invaders) should rule over them: wherefore should they say among the people, Where is their God?"* It would seem from the above scripture that the Temple will be rebuilt and Temple worship reestablished. It is the author's belief that this will occur in the near future.

In verses (18 to 21) the reader learns that Israel's enemies *"shall be a desolation...(while) Judah (Jews) shall dwell (that is continue to exist) forever, and from generation to generation."*

For I will cleanse their blood that I have not cleansed: for the Lord dwelleth in Zion." This cleansing of the Jewish people as a nation is a blessed promise that prepares them for the Tribulation and the wrath of the Antichrist.

Perhaps one other question that should be considered is that of Joel 2:4 which seems to picture the invaders riding horses. Those who interpret this literally suggest it will be easier for the invaders to come on horseback do to the difficult mountain terrain that separates Russia from Israel. This could also cause the attack to be one of surprise.

Hal Lindsay, in his book *Present world Events in the Light of Prophecy* (Voice of Healing Publishing Co., Shreveport, La.), suggests that a stamp, prepared in 1930, which pictures horsemen riding south by the Sea of Azov and the Black Sea in the direction of Israel is in a sense prophetic.

After the Lord predicts the defeat of the northern invaders, he declares that he will bless Israel with an outpouring of the Spirit (Joel: 2:23): twice that which was poured out on the Day of Pentecost, and described as both the *"former rain and the latter rain."* It is this great spiritual revival that brings the nation back to the Lord (and the acceptance of Jesus Christ as Messiah) and prepares them for an invasion <u>"by all nations,"</u> (Joel Chap. 3). This seems clearly to be the battle of Armageddon (Rev. 16:14-16). It should be noted that while Joel states the invaders are composed of "all nations," Rev. 16:14 refers to them as *" the kings of the earth and the whole world."*

To continue the study turn to Ezek. 37: 21-28. Here the Lord God promises Israel almost 600 years before their "scattering" among the nations (which began in 70 A.D.) that *"...Thus saith the Lord God; Behold, I will take the children of Israel from among the heathen, ... and will gather them on every side, and bring them into their own land; And I will make of them one nation... upon the mountains of Israel."*

the Russian stamp

In Ezek. 37: 1-4, the nation of Israel is presented as nation of "dry bones" in a Valley of Death. Then God tells Ezekiel to command the "four winds" to breathe upon the dead bones, which then come together and are clothed with muscles, flesh, skin, and receive the "breath of life" (v. 4). Then the prophet is told to prophesy to the now living and the "exceeding great army," whom God has brought out of their graves, that: I will *"... put my spirit in you, and ye shall live, and I shall place you in your own land: then ye shall know that I the Lord have spoken it, and performed it, saith the LORD (v.12-14)."*

This unique prophecy concerning Israel's return as an official nation and *"an exceeding great army"* of people was literally fulfilled in 1948. What is extremely important to realize is that the survival of Israel as a distinct people, and their restoration to their ancient homeland as predicted, was nothing that Israel or any other nation can take credit for, but was entirely the work of Almighty God.

In a sense this end time "trouble" began immediately after Israel declared herself an independent nation. This was on May 14, 1948. The next day five Arab armies attacked, the newborn nation in an attempt to destroy it in infancy. As history records, Israel won this initial phase of conflict; defeating Egypt from the south, Jordan from the east, as well as Syria, Lebanon and Iraq attacking from the north. Despite the pledge of the Arab world to "cast Israel into the sea," the onslaught (by the "seed of Ishmael" against the "seed of Isaac") fizzled out in less than a month; and so with the conflict of 1967. Despite the creation of the PLO (the Palestinian Liberation Organization) and the backing of Russia (supplying the Arabic nations with tanks and warplanes) the Six Day War left Israel in control of three times more land. This included the Old City of Jerusalem and the ancient Temple Mount. Though Israel returned some of the captured territories, Arab Jihad (holy war) continued with the "War of Attrition" in 1970 and the Yom Kippur War of 1973. Though victorious in both, the tiny Jewish nation experienced a growing number of military and civilian casualties as the PLO and other terror groups organized and launched multiple assaults on planes, busses, shopping malls: any place where both soldiers and civilians gathered. Over time the method of attack would go from incendiary bombs and rockets to human bombshells, some of the latter being young children. In 1972 PLO gunman would kill eleven young Israeli athletes at the Summer Olympic Games in Germany. In 1973 the Arab attack would include Americans. The U.S. Ambassador to the Sudan and a deputy were gunned down on what US intelligence would attribute to orders from Arafat. While this would be one of the first attacks on Americans it would certainly not be the last. The horrible reality and possible extent of such attacks on Americans would not "hit home" until the tragedy of 911. Only when bin Laden linked president Bush and the United States to a "Jewish plot to exterminate Muslims" did we comprehend "the why behind the hate". (Any friend of Israel is an enemy of radical Muslim Arabs.)

Since 1948 violent attacks on Israel have continued. As a result the decision was reached to build a security fence along the West Bank border in the hopes of repelling human bombers. This fence seems related to future prophecy that indicates it will be abandoned. This evidently due to a peace agreement between Israel and the PLO (Ezek. 38:11). This may come about due to possible US and EU intervention that will, bring, at the time, a sense of seeming peace in the Middle East. It should be noted that some may believe that the reason for Israel "dwelling safely" without walls, as described in Ezek. 38:11, refers to the time when (after the Rapture) Israel will make a covenant with the Antichrist. However, as pointed out, the forces destroyed by God Almighty in Ezek. Chap. 38 and 39 are not the nations of the world that are described as the enemy in Rev. Chap. 19:15."

In Ezek., Chapters 38 and 39, we are given more details related to the nation of Israel being invaded by this huge collective force from the north. The prophet Ezekiel addresses his message to Gog, the leader of the invaders, the chief prince of Meshech and Tubal and the land of Magog. Countries who accompany and assist Gog in this invasion are listed as Persia, Ethiopia, Libya, Gormer, and Togarmah. It is stated that this *"great company"* will, in *"the latter years,"* attack the people who have been *"gathered out of the nations"* which now *"dwell safely" without walls"(v. 11))*. Verses 9 & 10 tell us that the invaders will *"come like a storm... like a cloud to cover the land"* {as they} *"think an evil thought."*

The thought is: *"I will go up to the land of unwalled villages;"..(to them)... at rest, all of them dwelling safely, all of them dwelling without walls, {having} neither bars nor gates, To take a spoil, and to take a prey {booty}; to turn thine hand upon the desolate places that are now inhabited, and upon the people that are gathered out of the nations..."*(v.12 a).

While there is some difference of opinion among scholars as to the identity of Magog and the nations that accompany her in the invasion of Israel, many feel, as already suggested, that Magog is the ancient name for Russia, with Meshech and Tubal being ancient names for two of Russia's chief cities, Moscow and Tobolski. The nations accompanying Russia are thought to be Iran and some of the Arab states adjacent to Iran. These are Turkey and the central Asiatic peoples allied with Russia: Libya and Ethiopia." The author was impressed, as he wrote, by an article in the CANTON REPOSITORY (1-25-07) entitled: "Iran gets Russian air-defense missiles." This was reported by the Russian media stating: "Moscow...said it would supply 29 of the mobile surface-to-air missile systems to Iran under a 700million dollar contract signed in December 2005." As mentioned, modern day Iran is the Biblical Persia mentioned in Ezekiel 38:5 as being one of the invaders coming against Israel.

Surprisingly, no nations are listed as opposing the invaders with only a few questioning. These are SHEBA (remember the Queen of Sheba), DEDAN and the "young lions of TARSHISH." TARSHISH is believed to be Great Britain (England). Thus the young cubs are primarily the Untied States, Canada, and Australia. They only question (Ezek. 38:13), but they do nothing to come to the aid of Israel.

This, of course, is God's plan.. He wants Israel to know that ***HE IS THEIR ONE AND ONLY PROTECTOR!***

Some may ask what do the invaders hope to gain? The intent of the Satan inspired Muslim nations will be, as it has always been: the total destruction of Israel. The goal of Russia will be to "take a spoil" (v. 12). Without doubt, "the spoil" is not only the wealth of Israel, and its nuclear weapons, but control of all the Middle East and its oil.

Part Two: *The Climax To The Invasion*

The surprising and amazing result of the invasion is given in Ezek. 38 and 39. As many writers have expressed it, "The Lord will unleash the greatest earthquake in history: One that will be felt by *'all the men that are upon the face of the earth...the mountains shall be thrown down, and the steep places shall fall, and every wall shall fall to the ground..."* In the confusion the invaders will turn and fight each other, with only one sixth of the invading army escaping (39:6). As a result of this judgment, it will require seven months to bury the dead and seven years to burn up the confederation's weapons (39:9-12). (Evidently the steel in the weapons will be that which will melt under extreme heat.) What should also be considered is that this series of events possibly occurs before the seven year Tribulation begins, otherwise the nation of Israel, that is attacked and scattered by the Antichrist at the middle of the Tribulation, would not have "seven years" to spend gathering up and disposing of the weapons (Ezek. 39:9).

This divine intervention will cause many to repent (39:21-22). Even the Gentile nations will acknowledge God's power. The result of the devastation of Russia and her allies, will set the stage for the rebuilding of the temple (Ezek. 40) in Jerusalem and the rise of Antichrist as the head of a special, ten nation, European Union.

In addition to the defeat of the invading army, God sends "a fire" on Magog, and *"those that dwell carelessly in the isles."* Some scholars feel that at the time of the invasion, Russia will attempt to disable both Great Britain and the United States by the use of long range missiles or by missiles launched from off shore submarines. If this happens both the U.S. and Britain, along with Russia, will be reduced to second rate powers. This will leave the European Union the strongest political and military force in the world. It is, as the head of this Union, that Antichrist, the Satan incarnated dictator, will come to power. Soon after he will make a 7 year covenant of peace with Israel (Dan. (:27). But in the middle of it he will brake it by placing an image of himself in their holy temple (Mt. 24:15; Mk. 13:14; Dan. 11:31 & 12:11). He will then turn on God's chosen people in one last determined attempt to wipe them from the face of the earth and make Jehovah God a liar (Rev. 12:6, 13-17; Zech. 13:8-14:11; Jer. 31:7-11 & 31-37).

In view of the above truth, all–both Christian and non-Christians–should realize that the greatest sign that the world is nearing the end of this present age is: THE JEW BACK IN THE PROMISED LAND and SATAN TRYING TO DESTROY THEM! As Christians we should pray for the salvation of the Jewish people. Remember, all of this has come upon them because of their rejection of the Lord Jesus Christ as Messiah and Savior(Mt. 27:25). Psalm 122: 6 tells us: *"Pray for the peace of Jerusalem: they shall prosper that love thee."* As "watchmen upon the walls" we are commanded to give God *"no rest, till he establish, and till He make Jerusalem a praise in the earth"*(Isaiah 62:6). The Lord God has promised to answer both prayers: He promised Isaiah: *"thy people also shall be righteous: they shall inherit the land forever, the branch of my planting, the work of my hands, that I may be glorified. A little one shall become a thousand, and a small one a strong nation: I the LORD will hasten it in his time" (Isaiah 60:21-22).* The way things are going, God's time may be closer than we think! All that can be said for sure in relation to the time of this invasion is that it will follow a time of seeming peace, when Israel will have become "unwalled" (Ezek. 38: 8-11), and feel that they "dwell safely all of them." An ASSOCIATED PRESS story (12-

26-06) was headlined: "Israel Will Remove West Bank Roadblocks." It went on to say: "In JERUSALEM Israel agreed Monday to remove some of the military roadblocks that have hindered Palestinians in the West Bank....Israel's Prime Minister, Ehud Olmert, for the first time in more than a year, met with the Palestinian President: Mahmoud Abbas."

On 7-24-07 an Associated Press report read: "Arab\ League extends 'hand of peace' to Israel. The 22 member group sent a delegation to the Jewish state for the first time." The article went on to say: "Arab League envoys paid a historic visit to Israel…to present a plan calling for a regional treaty, saying they were extending an offer of peace to Israel on behalf of the Arab world."

The author wondered if this could be the beginning of an agreement or treaty that would result in Israel letting her "guard down" in fulfillment of Ezek. 38:11. When this happens the Gog attack, it seems, will be just around the corner!

As for the United States, it is certainly time to pray for an old fashioned, sincere, heart felt revival. We may well be one of the nations upon whom God sends " fire" because they "dwell carelessly" (Ezek.39:6). As suggested, it would seem that both Russia and the U.S. must cease to be major world powers in order for the revived Roman Empire to be supreme, and the Antichrist to be unchallenged.

What is interesting is that this is the only place in all of Scripture that there is any possible reference to the United States (one of the "young cubs" or offspring of the Merchants of Tarshish). One cannot help but wonder: Why is the United States, as powerful as we are now, not mentioned even once in the book of

Revelation, or any other of the Bible's prophecies? Will it have vanished from the face of the earth (like Sodom and Gomorrah), or simply rendered "not worth the mention?"

Chapter Six

Israel In the Tribulation Period

Scriptures such as 1st. Thess. 5:9 seem clearly to infer that the church will be delivered from the Wrath of the Tribulation period.

"For God hath not appointed us to wrath, but to obtain salvation by our Lord Jesus Christ.

Likewise 2nd Thess. Chap. Two gives additional verification that the Tribulation period and the reign of the Antichrist can not begin until the Body of Christ Church is removed. Paul begins by telling the Christians in Thessalonica not to believe reports that (due to much persecution) the *"day of Christ"* (the Day of the Lord's wrath) had already begun and they had not experienced their *"gathering together unto him"*(v.1). He goes on to on to say that the time of Tribulation will not come until the *"man of sin,"* (the Antichrist),*"the son of perdition,"* is *"revealed,"* and sits *"in the temple of God, showing himself that he is God (vs. 3-4)"*.

In Rev. Chap. 7:1-8, we are told of the sealing of the 144.00 "servants of God." The 144.000 are composed of 12,000 from each of the 12 tribes of Israel. The Tribes listed are: Judah, Ruben, Gad, Asher, Naphtali,

Manasseh, Simeon, Levi, Issachar, Zabulon, Joseph and Benjamin. Evidently they preach to the Jewish nation and the rest of the world for verse 9 declares:

> *"After this I beheld, and, lo, a great multitude, which no man could number, of all nations, and people, and tongues, stood before the throne, and the Lamb, clothed in white robes, and palms in their hands." (Rev.7:9)*

Evidently the preaching of the 144,000 brings results. Zech. 13 testifies to this.

"In that day there shall be a fountain opened to the house of David and to the inhabitants of Jerusalem for sin and uncleanness" (v.1). As a result the truth of Calvary will be made real as Christ appears unto them and reveals the wounds in his hands (v.6).

"And one shall say unto him, What are these wounds in thine hands? Then he shall answer, those with which I was wounded in the house of my friends."

The verses that follow seem to speak of the persecution of the nation by the Antichrist in which

> *"..in all the land, saith the Lord, two parts"* (two-thirds) *"shall be cut off and die, but the third part shall be left therein. And I will bring the third part through the fire, and will refine them as silver is refined, and will try them as gold is tried: they shall call on my name, and I will hear them: I will say, It is my people: and they shall say, The Lord is my God (v.8&9)."*

There has been much discussion as to how or where the *"third part"* will be protected from the wrath of the Antichrist, with many saying they will be hidden in a place called Petra. Actually all that can be known is found first in Revelation, Chapter Twelve. (A chapter filled with tremendous revelation.) Verses 1 to 6 (when linked to Gen. 37:4-10) tell of the Nation of Israel bringing forth a man child (who will rule all nations with a rod of iron) who is caught up to God and his throne (v. 5). Verses 3 and 4 tell of a *"great red dragon"* with *"seven heads and ten horns and seven crowns upon his heads."*

"And his tail drew the third part of the stars (angels) of heaven, and did cast them to the earth, and the dragon stood before the woman (Mary) which was ready to be delivered, for to devour her child as soon as it was born." The dragon, of course, is Satan. The "third part of the stars of heaven" looks back to the original rebellion that Satan led among the angels (Stars) of Heaven. The "ten horns and seven crowns" look forward to the Satan incarnated Antichrist (Rev.13:1; Isaiah 14:12-16).

To return to the question at hand: where will the children of Israel be hidden? Rev. 12:12:14-17 sheds a small amount of light, as does Dan.11: 40 and 41.

<u>*"And the woman (Israel) was given two wings of a great eagle, that she might fly into the wilderness, into her place, where she is nourished for a time, and times, and a half time,(3&1/2 years) from the face of the serpent.*</u> *And the serpent (the Antichrist) cast out of his mouth water as a flood after the woman, that he might cause her to be carried away by the flood. And the earth helped the woman, and the earth opened up her mouth, and swallowed up the flood which the dragon cast out of his*

mouth. And the dragon (Satan working in the Antichrist) was wroth with the woman, and went to make war with the remnant of her seed, which keep the commandments of God, and have the testimony of Jesus Christ "(Rev. 12:14-17).

The passage in Revelation appears to point to a wilderness area in, or close by, Israel. The passage in Daniel appears to specify Edom and Moab, which are south and west of Judah.

"He shall enter also into the glorious land, and many countries shall be overthrown: but these shall escape out of his hand, even Edom and Moab, and the chief of the children of Ammon." (Dan. 11:40-41)

Mark 13:14-19 seems to also speak of Israel's warning to flee and go into hiding when the Antichrist reveals himself by placing his image in the Temple (v. 14) Verse 15 relates the command of Christ: *"And let him that is in the housetop not go down into the house, neither enter therein, to take any thing out of his house: and let him that is in the field not turn back again for to take up his garment. But woe to them that are with child, and to them that suck in those days! And pray that your flight be not in winter. For in those days shall be affliction (for Israel), such as was not from the beginning of creation...."*

The purpose in their fleeing is to find a hiding place from the wrath of the Antichrist. Just where there could be such a hiding place today seems hard to understand, but with God all things are possible.

Chapter Seven

Where Will the Antichrist Come From? What Will Be His End?

The above questions are ones that many Bible believing Christians often ask. While numerous speculations have been offered, it seems a study of Daniel Chapter 7, 8, 9 and 11, along with Isaiah 10, 11, 14, and 30 are helpful.

In Daniel, Chap. 7, the kingdoms of Babylon (the lion), Medo-Persia (the bear), and Greece (the leopard) are followed by a nameless beast (the Roman Empire). Verses 7 and 8 look forward to the final form of the revived Roman Empire composed of ten nations. Here we are told in verse 8 that another "little horn" comes up among the ten horns and "plucks up," or destroys three of the ten horns. (Also see verses 15-27.)

In verse 25 of Isaiah 14 the Satan incarnated Anti-Christ, described in verses 1-20, is designated: *"the Assyrian."* Today Assyria lies east of Lebanon. and north of Jordan. In maps of the New Testament era it appears to have covered a much larger area. At the time of this writing, Muslims in the Middle East are looking for a reincarnation of Mohammad to appear on the scene. Perhaps, to them, the Antichrist, who will be slain and arise from the dead, will fulfill this expectation. (See Rev.13.)

That the prophecy of Isaiah 14 looks forward to the future seems apparent by the declaration that the satanic Antichrist, whose body will be denied ordinary burial (vs. 16-20), will be *"cast out"* and *"trodden under foot."* Not only will Israel be delivered but *the entire world* (the whole earth), "the Lord of hosts (Almighty God) hath determined this: *Who shall turn it back?"* God's judgment cannot be reversed. Verses 22 and 23 speak of Babylon, of whom the Lord says: "I *will sweep it with the bosom of destruction"*.... Whether these are a reference to a revived city (Ancient Babylon of Rev. 14:8; 16:19; and 18: 1-24), or the "great whore" of Rev. Chap. 17, or both, is a subject of interest.

"And there followed another angel saying, saying "Babylon is fallen, is fallen, that great city, because she made all nations drink of the wine of the wrath of her fornication (Rev. 14:8)."

"And upon her forehead was a name written, **MYSTERY, BABYLON THE GREAT, THE MOTHER OF HARLOTS AND ABOMINATIONS OF THE EARTH *(Rev.17:5)"*** (More later).

Aside from "Babylon", it seems apparent the Anti-Christ will be considered a native of Assyria.

What is also interesting is that Dan. 11:36-39 seems to suggest that the Antichrist may be a Jew who has denied the Jewish faith; though coming from Assyria, which is the home of both Muslims and several Middle East Christian denominations. That it refers to a denial of both Judaism and Christianity, the following verse seems clearly to imply.

" And the king shall do according to his will, and he shall exalt himself, and magnify himself above every god, and shall speak marvelous things against the God of gods (Jehovah God)....<u>Neither shall he regard the god of his fathers,</u> nor the desire of women, nor regard any god: for he will magnify himself above all. But in his estate shall he honor <u>the god of forces:</u> and a god whom his fathers knew not shall he honor with gold, and silver, and with precious stones, and pleasant things. Thus shall he do in the most strongholds with a strange god, whom he shall acknowledge and increase with glory: and shall cause them to rule over many, and shall divide the land for gain.".

Some believe "the god of forces" refers to a Fallen Angel who is used by Satan to assist the Antichrist in all of his activities. *(See the Expositor's STUDY BIBLE, edited by Jimmy Swaggart - p.1503, vs.38 & 39.)*

Fortunately, the reign of the Antichrist is limited. Rev. 19: speaks of the destruction of both the Antichrist and the false Prophet.

"And the beast was taken, and with him the false prophet that wrought miracles before him, with which he deceived them that had received the mark of the beast, and them that worshiped his image. These both were cast alive into a lake of fire burning with brimstone"(v.20).

"And the remnant were slain with the sword of him that sat upon the horse, which sword proceeded out of his mouth: and all the fowls were filled with their flesh" (v.21). Verses 11 to 16 tell us that the rider on the horse is the *"Word of God,"* the *"KING OF KINGS, AND LORD OF LORDS."*

In Chapter 20 Satan himself is bound by an angel and cast into "the bottomless pit" for "a thousand years (v.3)." Verse 4 presents the souls of those who refused to worship the beast or take his mark, living and reigning with Christ for a thousand years.

Verses 7and 8 tell of Satan's release ("out of his prison") from the bottomless pit and his gathering together of the nations from the four quarter's of the earth who *"compass the camp of the saints and the beloved city and fire came down from God out of heaven and devoured them."*

Verse 8 compares this defeat of the final Satan led rebellion to the previous battle of Gog and Magog: *"And he shall go out to deceive the nations which are in the four quarters of the earth, Gog and Magog, to gather them together to battle: the number of whom is as the sand of the sea."* These who are led in rebellion are, of course, those who are born during the 1000 year Millennium. Like Adam and Eve, before their fall, they are in a state of innocence. What lie it is that Satan uses to mislead them we are not told, but like Eve, they fall for it.

But let us return to the action of the Antichrist during the Tribulation.

Chapter-Eight

The Antichrist's Actions and God's Judgment!

Rev. Chapter Six is introduced by the "four beasts" of Rev. 4: 6-11 (undoubtedly angels). Verses,2-8 picture the reign of the Anti-Christ as one riding forth on a series of different colored horses. The first in verse 2 is a white horse.

"And I saw, and behold a white horse: and he that sat on him had a bow: and a crown was given unto him and he went forth conquering and to conqueror."

Evidently he is elected to the head of the Ten Nation League of Nations. As such, his initial program will be successful and quite appealing. Daniel Chapter 8 tells us: *"And his power shall be mighty, but not by his own power (but that of Satan's): and he shall destroy wonderfully, and shall prosper and practice, and shall destroy the mighty and the holy people. And <u>through his policy also he shall cause craft to prosper....</u>"* (Verses 24 - 25).

Riding the "white horse," it appears that he will bring about a tremendous boast in the economy of the entire world. Many will say: Surely, this cannot be an evil man!

Verse 25 continues: *"..and by peace (deceit) shall destroy many: he shall also stand up against the Prince of princes (the Lord Jesus Christ); but he shall be broken without hand"*

To return to Rev. Chapter 6, we see that the next horse the Anti-Christ rides is a "red one." On this horse he *"takes peace from the earth"* causing mankind to *"kill one another."*

As a means of killing those who oppose him, *"there is given unto him a great sword"(v.4)*. This sword, it seems, will be a huge and powerful United Nations army.

Verse 5 portrays the Antichrist on a *"black horse"* with *"a pair of balances (scales) in his hand."* By now the world economy has become one of "rationing," evidently due to a food shortage. Verse 6 reads: *"And I heard a voice in the midst of the four beasts say: 'A measure of wheat for a penny, and three measures of barley (horse feed) for a penny; and see thou hurt not the oil and the wine'."*

In verse 8 the reader sees a *"pale horse,"* whose rider is named "Death and Hell." It continues: *"And power was given unto them over a fourth part of the earth, to kill with sword, and with hunger, and with death and with the beasts of the earth."*

Verses 9-11 picture the souls of those (under the altar in heaven) who have been put to death by the Anti-Christ crying out to be *"avenged."* (Please note that these souls are not asleep in their graves, but are awake in heaven and seem to be aware of what is taking place on the earth.)

"And when he(Christ) had opened the fifth seal, I saw under the altar the souls of them that were slain for the word of God, and for the testimony which they held" (v.9). They are given *"white robes"* and told to *"rest (be patient) until their fellow servants...should be killed."* (v.10).

Verses 12 to 17 tell of a "great worldwide earthquake" which moves every mountain and island out of their places, causing every person on the face of the earth, from "kings" to "bond men," to go into hiding, crying out to the *"mountains and rocks, 'Fall on us, and hide us from the face of him that sitteth on the throne, and from the wrath of the Lamb: For the great day of his wrath is come; and who shall be able to stand?'"* (One cannot help but wonder why this will not bring world repentance?).

Revelation Chap. 13 continues with additional description of the Antichrist and his deception of mankind by a world government. In verse 1 we see this "beast," or government, coming out of "the sea." Evidently the " sea" represents the Gentile nations of the world over which this government will rule. In a sense, it is a combination of all the world empires that have existed in Europe and the Middle East.

"And I saw one of his heads as it were wounded to death; and his deadly wound was healed: and all the world wondered after the beast."

Many scholars believe this describes the amazing Satanic deception which will occur, resulting in worldwide worship of both Satan and the Antichrist. They say: *Who is like unto the Beast? Who is able to make war with him?" And there was given unto him a mouth speaking blasphemy against God, to blaspheme his name* *and his tabernacle (Jerusalem) and them that dwell in heaven. (The angels and the redeemed of all ages) And it was given unto him to make war with the saints, and to overcome them, and power was given him <u>over all kindreds, and tongues and nations.</u> And all that dwell upon the earth shall worship him, whose names are not written in the book of life of the Lamb slain from the foundation of the world."*

The great deception is an apparent restoration of the Antichrist to life after an apparent assassination. At this point Satan will feel he has defeated Christ and gained the control and worship of all mankind. However, the "patience and faith" of many who are saints will be demonstrated by their willingness to suffer martyrdom (v.10).

Chapter Nine

The False Prophet and The False Church

In order to assist the Antichrist in his deception, Satan provides a helper. Verses 11-18 of Rev. Cap. 13 give the details.

"And I beheld another beast coming up out of the earth; and he had two horns like a lamb, and spake as a dragon."

Here we see an individual who is empowered by Satan (the dragon) but pretends to be as "gentle as a lamb."

"And he exerciseth all the power of the first beast before him, and causeth the earth and them that dwell therein to worship the first beast, whose deadly wound was healed. And he doeth great wonders, so that he maketh fire come down from heaven on the earth in the sight of men, And deceiveth them that dwell on the earth by the means of those miracles which he had *power to do in the sight of the beast; saying to them that dwell on the earth that they should make an image to the beast.... And he had power to give life unto the image of the beast,*

that the image of the beast should both speak, and cause that as many as would not worship the image of the beast should be killed. And he causeth all, booth small and great, rich and poor, free and bond, to receive a mark in their right hand, or in their forehead: And that no man might buy or sell, save he had the mark, or the name of the beast, or the number of his name. Here is wisdom. Let him that hath understanding count the number of the beast: for it is the number of a man; and his number is six hundred threescore and six (666)."

The "second beast," referred to by many scholars as "the false prophet," gives life and power to the image of the beast to: *"both speak, and cause that as many as would not worship the beast (that they) should be killed."*

In the past the humanizing of this second beast would have seemed quite miraculous. At the time of this writing an article in USA TODAY (11-29-07) gives both a picture and an account of a human like female robot that not only has what appears to be human flesh, but also cries like a human when she suffers pain.

The article states: *The dental-training robot, dubbed Simroid for "simulator humanoid," has realistic skin, eyes and a mouth fitted with replica teeth that (dental) students practice drilling on. A sensor fitted where the nerve endings would be, raises an alert when they drill too close - triggering a yelp from the robot: "Ow, that hurt!"*

It seems the means of causing the "image of the beast" to at least "speak," has already been perfected. To be able to give additional commands is probably just around the corner, if not already a reality.

As Christians we certainly look forward to being in the rapture (the catching up to Heaven) and not having to face the the Antichrist and the loss of life when we refuse to take "his mark."

Of course a great many saved during the Tribulation will have to do so, as they refuse to honor the Antichrist (Rev. 7:9-17). Verse 9 tells the reader there will be a "great multitude" *which no man could number, of all nations, and kindreds, and people and tongues (who will, as a result, stand) before the throne, and before the Lamb (Christ) clothed with white robes, and palms intheir hands."* They cry with a *"loud voice, saying, 'Salvation to our God, which sitteth upon the throne, and unto the Lamb.'"* As previously mentioned Rev. 6:12-16 speaks of a great earthquake that causes mankind to hide themselves in "the dens and rocks of the mountains," asking these to *"hide us of the Lamb. This same earthquake is mentioned in Isaiah 2:12-22.* Verse 12 declares: *"For the day of the Lord of hosts shall be upon every one that is proud and lofty, and upon every one that is lifted up; and he shall be brought low."*

In Rev. 16:18-21 the same, or a similar, earthquake is mentioned. In addition verse 19 speaks of a "great Babylon." It reads:

"And the great city was divided into three parts, and the cities of the nations fell, and great Babylon came in remembrance before God, to give unto her the cup of wine of the fierceness of his wrath."

In chapter 17 Babylon is pictured as *"a great whore that sitteth upon many waters: with whom the kings of the earth have committed fornication, and the inhabit-*

ants of the earth have been made drunk with the wine of her fornication." So he carried me away in the spirit (divine revelation)...and I saw a woman sit upon a scarlet colored beast, full of names of blasphemy, having seven heads and ten horns....And upon her forehead was a name written, MYSTERY, BABYLON THE GREAT, THE MOTHER OF HARLOTS AND ABOMINATIONS OF THE EARTH. And I saw the woman drunken with the blood of the saints, and with the blood of the martyrs of Jesus..."(v.1-6)

"And here is the mind that hath wisdom. The seven heads are seven mountains, on which the woman sitteth"(v. 9).

These "seven mountains" are felt to be the seven hills on which the Vatican is located. The "blood of the saints and martyrs" seems clearly to be that of the many Protestants put to death by Catholic authority in past centuries.

In addition to the scriptures previously quoted, Rev. 14:8 and 16:19 speak of Babylon as a literal city. Rev. 14:8 states: *"And there followed another angel saying, Babylon is fallen, is fallen, that great city, because she made all nations drink of the wrath of her fornication."*

Rev. 16:19 *states: "And the great city was divided into three parts, and the cities of the nations fell: and great Babylon came in remembrance before God, to give her the cup of the wine of the fierceness of his wrath."*

That Babylon is not just a literal city is made plain by the scriptures listed above, that speak of "Mystery Babylon." The fact that she rides the back of the Beast as he comes to power (Rev. 17:7) and is later made "desolate (destroyed)" by the ten horns that are "upon the beast" (Rev. 17:16) tells the reader that she (the woman

drunken with the blood of the saints and martyrs of Jesus) is much more than just an ordinary city. If "the woman" is not the Catholic church, one can only wonder just who she is? Certainly no other religious group has such political power and world-wide influence as Catholicism! Nor has any other religious organization such a past record of the persecution of those who reject her teachings. To all readers who may be Catholic, the author would ask you to please be sure that you have put your trust in the finished work of Christ alone for your salvation. Do not depend on "confession, baptism, or any other religious ordinance" for salvation. And we would say the same to members of all other Christian denominations: be sure you have acknowledged your self to be a sinner and have accepted Christ's death on Calvary as the payment for your sin. If you will do this in sincerity, God will fill your heart with the peace of forgiveness and the witness of His Spirit that you are His child! If Catholic, or Protestant, it is not a denomination but the Lord Jesus Christ that saves. Above all, read and study the Scripture every day. The doctrines of every denomination, Catholic, Protestant, or other should be examined in the light of Scripture.

Chapter Ten

Signs of the End

At the time of this writing numerous signs have occurred with others seemingly on the verge of occurrence. Among these are storms such as Katrina, the War in Iraq and U.S. controversy with both Iran and Russia. What is also reality (forgotten by many) is the European Union with its "common currency." While the EU, as yet, is more than a ten nation union, this final, biblical prophetic form, may not be far off. Also prophetic is that which has been proposed by Israel: the rebuilding of the Temple (Ezekiel Chap. 40). Since the Muslims still occupy this ancient holy site, the defeat of Gog may have to occur first. As pointed out, this attack on Israel could occur at any time.

In addition another universal catastrophe seems already in the making. A 2-3-07 article in the Canton Repository entitled: "Global Warming Unstoppable for Centuries; Scientists Hoping for Fast Government Action," warns about "dire consequences" that could possibly occur. "The worst could be "more than one million dead and hundreds of billions of dollars in costs by 2100, in a world adapting to more extreme weather such as droughts, hurricanes, and wildfires."

While the year 2100 seems a long way off, there is no evidence that these catastrophic events could not occur much sooner. At any rate it sounds much like predictions from the Gospels and the Book of Revelation. In Luke 21:10 and 11 Jesus said: *"...Nation shall arise against nation, and kingdom against kingdom: And great earthquakes shall be in divers places, and famines and pestilences; and fearful sights and great signs shall there be from heaven."* The warning is repeated in verses 25-28. In verse 27 we are told: *"And then shall they see the Son of man coming in a cloud with power and great glory. And when these things begin to come to pass, ... look up for your redemption draweth nigh."* In verse 32 Jesus declares: *"...This generation* (the one in which they commence) *shall not pass away, till all be fulfilled."* Verse 34 adds: *"And take heed to yourselves, lest at anytime your hearts be overcharged with surfeiting and drunkenness, and cares of this life, and so that day come upon on you unawares. For as a snare shall it come on all them that dwell on the face of the whole earth."* These verses seem to speak clearly of events that will occur before the Rapture and the judgments of the Tribulation as described in Rev. 6:12-17.

At the time of this writing both TV and the newspaper tell of numerous hurricanes killing many and leaving thousands of homes destroyed as well as tremendous earthquakes and flooding in America and around the world. Every day it seems more end time predictions are coming to pass!

Perhaps one of the most significant signs is the birth of the reality and use of implanted "radio ID tags."

An article in the Canton Repository (7-25-07) entitled "Chipping America," relates how their use has become a "new battleground." About 7-25-06 two workers were "chipped"(embedded) with these identification tags, which are as long as two grains of rice and as thick as a toothpick, as a means of restricting access to vaults that held "sensitive data and images for police departments." Without the implants they could not open the vault doors.

The article goes onto say that the use of such chips has fired up protest with the fear "that the government, or your employer, might someday say: Take a chip or starve!" In addition "some critics (see) the implants as the fulfillment of a biblical prophecy that describes an age of evil in which humans are forced to take the 'mark of the Beast' on their bodies to buy or sell anything." (See Rev. Chap.13:16-17) Implantations are said to be "...quick, relatively simple procedures. After a local anesthetic is administered, a large-gauge, hypoder- mic needle is injected midway between the arm and the shoulder."

One wonders: If the means of the "mark of the Beast" has become a present reality, how close are we to the appearance of the "Beast" (the Antichrist) himself? We will consider this thought in the following chapter.

Dear Reader Friend, If you have not as yet repented of your sin and accepted Jesus Christ as your Savior and Lord, please do so today! As we hope to show in the following chapter, the appearance of the Antichrist and the Tribulation Period may be much closer than we realize.

Chapter Eleven

Is the Antichrist Alive Today?

The chapter title speaks of a question often asked by students of Bible Prophecy: Could the Antichrist be alive today? In view of the events presented in the previous chapter it would seem that these are truly the last days and mankind is on the verge of the Tribulation period. Thus the Antichrist could very well be alive. If he is the one referred to in Isa. 14:25: *"...I will break the Assyrian in my land (the land of Israel), and upon my mountains tread him under foot...."*, then perhaps Christians should keep an eye on Assyria, as well as the European Union.

In addition to the above end time signs, a recent vote by Congress appears to have endorsed a standardized, electronically readable driver's license that could possibly usher in a national ID card. These cards, or the lack of them, would curb access to everything from airplanes and trains to national parks and some courthouses (c/net NEWS. com.). One wonders: Could this be groundwork for the coming "mark of the Beast" (Rev. 13:16-18)?

Related scriptures in Rev. 13 tell us that the "mark of the beast," when it becomes reality, will be set in force by a false prophet who is presented in Rev. 13:11 as having "two horns" like a {gentle} lamb, but will {speak as a dragon}. That is Satan will use him as a powerful mouth piece.

"And he exerciseth all the power of the first beast before him, and causeth the earth and them which dwell therein to worship the first beast, whose deadly wound was healed. **(The Antichrist is evidently put to death by an assassin, but his "deadly wound" is "healed," as he is miraculously restored to life.)**

The false prophet continues his deception by calling down "fire from heaven" and performing other miracles (v.13 & 14). He commands an image to be made of the Antichrist, to which he "gives life" and the ability to speak. As a result the image commands that any who do not worship it are to be put to death (v.15). Verses 16-18 tell us:

> *"And he causeth all, both small and great, rich and poor, free and bond, to receive a mark in their right hand, or in their forehead. And that no man might buy or sell, save he had the mark, or the name of the beast, or the number of his name. Here is wisdom. Let him that hath understanding count the number of the beast: for it is a number of a man; and his number is six hundred threescore and six (666)."*

In Rev. 14: 9-11, because of his love for mankind, the Lord sends an angel "with a loud voice" of warning:

"If any man worship the beast and his image, and receive his mark in his forehead, or in his hand, the same shall drink of the wine of the wrath of God, which is poured out without mixture into the cup of his indignation, and he shall be tormented with fire and brimstone in the presence of the holy angels, and in the presence of the Lamb. And the smoke of their torment ascendeth up forever and forever: and they have no rest day nor night, who worship the beast and his image, and whosoever receiveth the mark of his name."

A Final Summary

In closing it would seem there are several very important events for which Christians should be looking. One is that for which the Iranian President, Mahound Ahmadinejah, is said to be looking. This is the return of the Muslim Messiah, "the Mahdi." He will lead the fight against Israel and the corrupt Western world, and conqueror the world for Allah (the true God). Jack Chick in his newsletter, *Battle Cry,* (March/April 2006) related how extensive has been the effort to promote this belief among Muslims: "He has all Iran buzzing about the return of the Mahdi. Children's magazines and school curricula contain teachings about his appearance. A messiah hot line and news agency solely dedicated to the latest developments have been set up." As we have shown, Scripture seems clearly to declare that the Antichrist will rise to power in the Middle East. Certainly the Muslims are looking for their Messiah!

As mentioned, a second key prophetic sign is that of Russian support of Iran. An article in the CANTON REPOSITORY, Jan. 25th, 2007, entitled "Iran gets Russian air-defense missiles," tells of Russia's claim to have recently supplied Iran with Tor-M1 missiles, this under a 700 million dollar contract signed in December of 2006. It seems to this author that this is one more step in preparation for the Russian, Muslim attack on Israel, and possibly the US, as described in this book's section about Gog and Magog.

Finally a third prophetic sign is the fact that far too many Christians and churches seem to be living in the period of the of the last, or seventh Church of Laodicea. In verses 15 -22 of Revelation, Chapter Three, the words of Christ in summary are:

"I know thy works, that thou art neither cold nor hot. So then because thou art lukewarm, and neither cold nor hot, I will spue thee out of my mouth. Because thou sayest, I am rich, and increased with goods, and have need of nothing, and knowe not that thou art wretched, and miserable, and poor, and blind, and naked (spiritually): I counsel thee to buy of me gold tried in the fire that thou mayest may be rich; and white raiment, that thou mayest be clothed that the shame of thy nakedness do not appear, and anoint thine eyes with eyesalve, that thou mayest see. As many as I love, I rebuke and chasten: be zealous therefore and repent Behold I stand at the door and knock: if any man hear my voice, and open the door, I will come in to him, and will sup with him, and he will sup with me. To him that overcometh will I grant to sit with me in my throne, even as I also overcame, and am set down with my Father in his throne. He that hath an ear, let him hear what the Spirit sayeth to the churches."

What a wonderful promise to those who will obey and ask the Holy Spirit to set them on fire with a burden for the lost and a desire to please Jesus, their Wonderful Lord! The final event for which all children of God should be praying is a mighty, God sent, world-wide revival. Let all who are true believers, ask the Lord to help us do all that we can to spread His Word. We should never forget the promise of Psalm 126: 5 and 6:

"They that sow in tears shall reap in joy. He that goeth forth and weepeth, bearing precious seed, shall doubtless come again with rejoicing, bringing his sheaves with him."

The author and his wife: Jim and Joan Ford

www.ingramcontent.com/pod-product-compliance
Ingram Content Group UK Ltd.
Pitfield, Milton Keynes, MK11 3LW, UK
UKHW041955230426
12048UKWH00008B/350